walk awhile in *my* shoes

gut-level, real-world messages
from employees to managers

Eric Harvey and Steve Ventura

based on the inner thoughts of hundreds of employees
shared in discussions over an eighteen-year period

To order additional copies of **walk awhile in *my* shoes**
or for information on other
WALK THE TALK® resources and initiatives,
please contact us at
1.888.822.WALK (9255)

THE WALK THE TALK COMPANY

Published by: Performance Publishing Company, a subsidiary of
Performance Systems Corporation
2925 LBJ Freeway, Suite 201
Dallas, Texas 75234

Performance Publishing books may be purchased for educational, business, or sales promotional use.

WALK THE TALK® is a registered trademark of Performance Systems Corporation.

Cover photograph by Keith Bardin. Cover design by Powell Design Office.

Printed in the United States of America.
20 19 18 17 16 15 14 13 12 11

ISBN 1-885228-28-7

Acknowledgement

Special thanks to Al Lucia for providing the insight, experience, and encouragement that helped turn the idea of this book into a reality.

Do not judge
any man
until you have walked
two moons
in his moccasins.

— Native American saying

Dear Manager:

I am every employee, and I work in every part of this organization. My collar is blue, pink, and white ... and frequently stained with the sweat that comes with hard work.

I am man, and I am woman. I'm every color, every belief, and every size. I'm old, young, and everything in between. I've worked here longer than you and not as long as you. I am a daughter. I am a son. I'm married and single, a parent and without children. I'm alone and I'm surrounded by people I care about deeply.

Sometimes you may think of me as only a number, or perhaps just another small cog in a very large wheel that you have to manage. But like you, I am a human being filled with joys, fears, frustrations, and hopes. I feel, I laugh, and I hurt. And, like you, I want to be understood, accepted, and appreciated.

The following pages are about opening up to you — about sharing my feelings on just a few of the many aspects of my job and how they affect me. Some of what you read may surprise you … some may bring a laugh or two. All of these pages, I hope, will encourage you to see me in a new and perhaps much different light.

I ask that you receive these messages with the same level of compassion and understanding that you wish from me as I read the flip side of this book. Chances are we're not as different as you may think. And just maybe … you'll be more inclined to "meet me in the middle," where we can begin a new and better working relationship.

Hear me. Understand me.

Walk awhile in *my* shoes.

On "change"

Okay, I admit it. When it comes to change, one of my first thoughts tends to be: "I wish you'd make up your mind!" One day you want me to do *this*, the next day it's *that* … and sometimes it's both this *and* that on the *same* day.

Change is particularly tough on me because when it gets "rolling downhill," guess who's usually standing at the bottom of the hill? Me! I'm rarely the "decider," but almost always the "doer." Seems like I no sooner get comfortable and proficient with my job and WHAM! — a whole new set of requirements and expectations are dropped on me. I *do* like feeling that I'm making a contribution to this organization. But it's getting harder and harder to feel that way.

Like you, I'm learning that continuous change and life are one and the same. But some changes are a lot easier to swallow than others. I'm basically okay with doing things differently to keep up with our competitors. But I do reject those changes that are sometimes required because you screwed up and didn't think things through. Maybe if you asked my opinion a little more often, that wouldn't happen.

My biggest problem with change comes when you don't take the time to explain **why**! If you know why, tell me, and you'll increase the odds that I'll support what has to be done. If you don't know why, **try to find out!**

I'm struggling with this new business environment of ours. I'm doing the best I can, but I'm scared. A little more sensitivity and patience on your part will go a long way toward helping me cope.

Change may not be easy for you, but at least you're calling some of the shots. Try walking awhile in *my* shoes!

Sometimes I feel like I'm standing at the corner of WALK and DON'T WALK!

— Unknown

On recognition

I've been known to say, "I don't want any pats on the back — just put it in my check." Well, don't believe it. It's a crock! Regardless of how I may act, I do care a great deal what you and others think of me and what I do. Recognition *is* important to me. That's why I wear award pins, belt buckles, and the like; that's why I display trophies in my home; that's why I hang certificates on my wall.

Believe it or not, I'm looking for more from this job than just a paycheck. There's got to be more, 'cause I'm sure not gonna get rich on what I make! What *do* I want? I want to feel good about myself and the work I do; I want to feel like I really am an important part of this organization. And I tend to gauge my self-worth by others' perceptions ... I often see myself through *your* eyes.

I fully realize that I don't do great work all the time. Some days I hit the bull's-eye, some days I'm in the outer rings, and once in a while, I miss the target altogether. I don't expect you to see me as a top-notch performer all the time. But I do expect to be periodically recognized when I either go above and beyond the call of duty or just maintain good, solid performance over a long period of time. And the more you recognize my good work, the more good work I want to do. It's funny the way that works. I think it's all part of "human nature."

I know you're often so busy you probably don't think about recognizing me. And maybe you sometimes figure you don't get recognition yourself, so why should you give it to others? But if you'll just make a greater effort to let me know you appreciate me, I'll do my best to reciprocate. And I promise I won't complain about receiving too much praise!

Please understand how important this is to me. Walk awhile in *my* shoes.

On performance evaluations

From my perspective, both the *best* and the *worst* thing about performance evaluations is that they usually only happen once a year. Why best? Because they tend to be tedious and sometimes painful processes — similar to annual trips to the dentist. Why worst? Because all too often, they're the *only* time I get any detailed feedback on how well I am (or am not) doing. And sometimes even that doesn't happen "constructively."

Evaluations represent scary-land for me because they are *subjective* in nature. Your opinion is going to affect my future. And there are no guarantees that one evaluator (and most of the time it is just *one* evaluator) really knows my job and how well I do it. So sometimes I can't help but worry that my rating will be based solely on how well you like me. I worry you'll forget the good and remember only the bad. And I worry that my input won't be considered in the process.

I understand that performance evaluations probably aren't the most favorite part of your job. But they *are* important to me … I've got a lot riding on them. If all you can do is call it like you see it, then please make sure you look hard enough to see the true picture.

And as you're looking, maybe you could consider periodically giving me a little more *informal* feedback — the kind where there's not so much on the line. Make it constructive, and I'll do my best to receive it constructively.

Have strong feelings about performance evaluations? Walk awhile in *my* shoes!

When you point
your finger at me,
remember that
three of your fingers
are pointing back
at you!

— Louis Nizer
(adaptation)

On "participative management"

All things considered, I do a pretty decent job of managing my own life. I vote and I pay taxes. I obey the laws (most of them, anyway). I dress and feed myself and probably others as well. I pay bills. I manage a checking account. I plan vacations. The list goes on and on. **I am a responsible adult with a brain!** But sometimes at work I feel I'm treated like I can't think or be trusted to make good decisions. It happens more than you might imagine, and it bothers me as much as it would bother you.

Believe it or not, I do keep up with certain trends. I know that concepts like "participative management," "teams," and "empowerment" are part of today's business scene. And I understand how they can help make businesses better and more successful. Sometimes I see those trends happening in our organization — I see employees being given the opportunity to provide input on key decisions and work processes. Sometimes I don't.

I understand that these trends may not be easy for you to accept and deal with. They probably aren't the way things were done when you came up through the ranks. And they may involve many hurdles that I'm not aware of and therefore can't truly appreciate. I just know that sometimes the chance to participate seems real, sometimes it's token, and sometimes it's non-existent.

Here's what else I know: It's a lot easier to feel like an important part of this organization when I have the chance to become involved; it's a lot easier to hear words like "act like you own the business" when you give me the opportunity to do so. Remember that I've got a stake in this organization's success just like you do.

Even as a manager, ever feel that you'd like a little more say in how things are done around here? Try walking awhile in *my* shoes!

I don't care to be
involved in the
crash landing
unless I can be in
on the takeoff.

— Harold Stassen

On how performance problems are dealt with

When it comes to dealing with performance problems, I don't envy you a bit. It's got to be one of the biggest pains in the rear you face. You see, I've been there. Although my experiences have mostly been away from the job, I still know what it's like to deal with "people problems." It's a tough thing to do. (Being on the receiving end is no walk in the park either!) And at work, it's a subject I have strong feelings about — mostly on *how* and *when* it's done.

If I screw up, I don't expect you to overlook it. Just treat me with respect, deal with the facts, consider my side, and give me a chance to correct the problem. And please, don't wait for me to get into deep weeds before you talk with me. The sooner you bring it up, the sooner I can fix it. Generally, how I respond will be determined by how you deal with me. Talk to me like an adult, and I'll most likely respond in kind. If I don't, I'm "the heavy," not you ... and I've bought any consequences I get.

Just as I don't expect *my* problems to be overlooked, I don't expect the problems of my co-workers to be overlooked either. Here's something you may not realize: Nothing ticks me off more than to see management look the other way while people around me "get away with murder" — especially when I have to pick up the slack and carry their part of the load. It's unfair and I resent it. And my resentment will eventually show up in the quality and quantity of my work.

Perhaps there are times when you feel like a "victim" of performance problems. If so, you're not alone. Want some company? Walk awhile in *my* shoes.

TO ORDER

📞 **1.888.822.WALK (9255)**

📠 **972.243.0815**

Ask about our other high high-impact publications:

- ◆ *Walk The Talk ... And Get The Results You Want*
  The best-selling business book that shows leaders, at all levels, why and how to turn organizational values into value-added practices.

- ◆ *144 Ways To Walk The Talk*
  The quick-reference handbook packed with practical ideas and strategies for practicing values-driven leadership.

- ◆ *Walking The Talk Together*
  The powerful handbook that encourages all employees to take responsibility for values-driven business practices.

- ◆ *Forget For Success*
  The practical, easy-read that pinpoints counterproductive beliefs and people practices which negatively impact your culture and bottom line.

For information on these and other values-based business resources, visit our website:

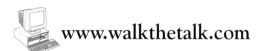 **www.walkthetalk.com**

Values **B**ased **B**usiness **S**olutions

The WALK THE TALK® Company
2925 LBJ Freeway, Suite 201, Dallas, Texas 75234-7100
972.243.8863 ‣ Fax 972.243.0815 ‣ www.walkthetalk.com

Walk Awhile In *MY* Shoes
Order Form

**Client
Priority Code**
86R2

1-99	$6.95 each		
100-999	$6.45 each	Copies	_____
1000-4999	$5.95 each		
5000-9999	$5.45 each	Book Total $	_____
10,000 or more	$4.95 each		

Shipping and Handling* +$ _____

Subtotal $ _____

Texas Only   Sales Tax (8.25% of Subtotal) $ _____

TOTAL $ _____

*SHIPPING & HANDLING CHARGES:

Order $ Amount	Charges
Up to $50	$4
$50-99	$7
$100-249	$10
$250-649	$18
$650-1,299	$32
$1,300-1,999	$55
$2,000-3,499	$68

Outside the continental U.S., please call.

Orders shipped ground delivery to be received in 7-10 business days. Next business day and second business day delivery is available. Please call for information.

☐ YES, I want more information on WALK THE TALK® Workshops, Consulting, and 360° Profile Services to help my organization turn values into value-added results. Please send me a free WALK THE TALK® RESOURCES Catalog.

Name (MR/MS) _____

Title _____

Organization _____

Street Address _____

City _____ State _____ Zip _____ Country _____

Phone (____) _____ Ext. _____ (required to process order)

Fax (____) _____ E-mail _____

Purchase Order Number (if applicable) _____

☐ MasterCard   ☐ VISA   ☐ AMERICAN EXPRESS Cards   ☐ Check or Money Order Enclosed (Payable to: The WALK THE TALK Co.)   ☐ Please Invoice (orders over $100 only)

Account Number _____ Expiration Date _____
(month/year)

Signature _____

Prices effective January 1, 1998 are subject to change without notice. Orders payable in U.S. dollars only. Orders outside U.S. and Canada must be prepaid by credit card or check drawn on a U.S. bank. Orders under $100 must be prepaid by credit card, check, or money order. Restocking fee on returns within 30 days of original receipt. THANK YOU FOR YOUR ORDER.

On "no win" situations

Ever wrestle with the question: "How do I motivate my employees?" Well, I've got a suggestion I think will help. STOP TRYING! Instead, spend your time getting rid of the things that *de*-motivate me. And one of the top items on that list is "no win" situations.

If you've ever felt like you just can't win no matter what you do, you know what a lousy feeling it is. And it's something I experience more often than you might think. The plain fact is that there are times when I do what I'm supposed to do, and, BOOM, I get nailed for it.

Sometimes you suggest I do things like "show more initiative instead of waiting to be told everything." So I give it a try ... I take the bull by the horns. But if it turns out bad, what happens? You get on my case for not checking with you first! BOOM, I lose.

Then there are times when I get punished for good performance. I bust my tail and do a good job handling tough tasks or problems, while some of my peers are goofing off or doing just enough to get by. So what happens the next time there's a tough job? I get stuck with it. BOOM, I lose again. And, if I happen to screw up that next tough job? You guessed it: BOOM!

I know (at least I hope) that these actions are unintentional on your part. But that doesn't diminish the level of frustration I feel. I want to do a good job, and I want to "win" when I do. If I face too many "no win" situations, I'll eventually stop trying to win. Then, BOOM, we both lose.

Please think about this. Walk awhile in *my* shoes.

Be nice to people on your way up.
You might need them on the way down.

— Jimmy Durante

On resolving
disputes

Call them complaints, grievances, disputes, whatever — the name really doesn't matter. Because I'm human, it's inevitable that I occasionally have concerns about how I'm treated at work. Sometimes my issues get resolved, or they work themselves out. But other times I just end up living with them. They affect my work, and they play a big role in shaping how I view you and the organization.

Chances are you boast of having an "open door policy," where I can come in and discuss my concerns "at any time." I appreciate the good intentions such a policy represents. But I don't think you realize how difficult it can be to step through that door. Sometimes I find that you're just too busy to give me the attention I feel I deserve. For you, it may be just another problem, or perhaps just another "whiny employee." For me, it's a very important issue that's probably been bothering me for some time.

It's especially difficult to come to you when *you* are the cause of my concern. I end up having to go to "the person who done me wrong" in order to get resolution. Who wouldn't be uncomfortable with that? Who wouldn't fear being labeled a "trouble maker"? Who wouldn't fear the possibility of retribution? So, sometimes I just shut up (at least around you) and take it.

There's a catch-22 here that I don't know how to stop. You validly have a right to ask, "How can I possibly resolve employee complaints if I don't know they exist?" But I also must ask, "How can I be expected to use a process I fear — or at least have little confidence in?" I wish I had an answer to recommend, but I don't. I only have concerns.

Think dispute resolution is a tough nut to crack? Try walking awhile in *my* shoes!

On sharing information

Remember the childhood dig, "I know something you don't know"? I remember it well. I learned at an early age that **knowledge is power**. And as I've grown up (or at least grown older), I've found that things haven't changed — especially at work. Now I frequently find myself thinking, "You know something I don't know." And that thought bothers me. It makes me feel like a kid again — in a negative sense.

Be it correct or not, my perception is that management often knows a lot more about our business than they're telling. I certainly understand that not all information is for public consumption. Some things must be kept confidential. Even I have dealings with you that I don't want others to know about. But sometimes you take a parental, "they don't need to know" approach with non-confidential data. Or even worse, you assume, "they don't want to be bothered with all this stuff."

Here's a suggestion: How about letting *me* be the judge of what I need or want to know about? I may be interested in more than you think! When you get information on our organization's performance, financial picture, quality statistics, etc., pass them along. Let me know about future plans for expansion into new products and services. Share information about our competition and trends in our industry. If I throw it in the trash, that's my choice. At least you'll have made an effort to make me feel like I'm an important part of this business.

And by all means, don't feel like you have to protect me from bad news. I'm an adult; I can take it. Hearing bad news isn't pleasant, but it's no worse than being left in the dark … and assuming the worst.

Maybe you sometimes feel like you don't know everything that's going on around here. If so, try walking awhile in *my even more* uninformed shoes.

The best
mind-altering drug is
truth.

— Lily Tomlin

On respecting my time

So much work, so little time! If you've ever felt there's just not enough time in the day to get your work done, you're not alone. I may not work long hours as frequently as you, and yes, I do sometimes take off as soon as my shift ends. But that doesn't make my time any less valuable than yours.

I've got a job to do, and you expect me to do it well. Part of my job involves doing things you need done. Many times you expect me to drop whatever I'm doing in order to meet your needs. That's okay if the tasks to be done are *truly* important. But I get frustrated when you take a "top priority" approach with *every* assignment. Sometimes I'm still in the middle of one "do it now" when you give me another one. And somewhere in all that, I'm expected to do my regular work, too.

Ask me what I'm working on *before* you give me an assignment, and I'll be much more likely to believe that my work truly is important. Ask if I have a few minutes to discuss your needs instead of walking up and telling me what to do, and I'll be much more inclined to believe that time is a precious resource that must be respected and used wisely. Act like my time isn't important, and I'll resent it. Even worse, I just might follow your lead.

Ever feel your management time isn't always respected? Try walking awhile in *my employee* shoes!

On "loyalty" and job security

It used to be that if you worked hard, kept your nose clean, and were loyal to the company, you were pretty much assured of a job for life ... or at least as long as you wanted it. No more! I read the papers and watch the evening news. I see a growing amount of evidence that job security is becoming a thing of the past. The "guarantees" our parents and grandparents enjoyed (or at least thought they enjoyed) are disappearing. And that's frightening. It plays games with my mind. I feel like I'm running scared a lot.

When I hear terms like "restructuring," "re-engineering," "buy-out," "merger," "downsizing," etc., I can't help but wonder if they will happen here. I worry how they might affect me. That's natural ... I'm only human. And quite frankly, it's an awful thing to have hanging over your head. I try not to think about it and just do my job, but it's hard.

I bet *you* share many of these same fears. It's obvious that managers are no more immune to changing trends than employees are. I hope that you'll be as sensitive to my concerns as you want others to be to yours.

If there are times when you feel I need to be more loyal to you and the company, please understand that I'm struggling to define what "loyalty" means in today's ever-changing business world. Like you, I'm searching for some degree of stability — something I can hold on to — in what seem to be unstable times.

And if you could find some way to reassure me that hard work *does* pay off, I'd really appreciate it. It's getting harder and harder to believe. But I *do* want to believe it.

Understand my fears. Walk awhile in *my* shoes.

The best executive is the one who has enough sense to pick good people to do what he wants done, and self-restraint enough to keep from meddling with them while they do it.

— Theodore Roosevelt

On the joys
of the job

Before you go assuming this book is nothing more than a "woe is me" lament, let me set the record straight. There are many positive aspects to my job. Here's a list of just a few of the workplace "turn-ons" I experience:

- Doing good work that I can be proud of ... and being recognized and appreciated for it.

- Having my ideas on how to improve the business taken seriously ... and occasionally adopted. I really like it when you ask, "What do you think?"

- Having you trust my work ethic and competency enough that you don't feel the need to constantly look over my shoulder.

- Being respected as a decent employee, and, more importantly, a decent person.

- Being part of a team in which everyone pulls together and carries his or her share of the load.

- Making a contribution — feeling that things came out different and better because I was involved.

- Achieving an adequate balance between my job and my personal life.

When it comes to the above, I'm guessing you feel the same way. No doubt you've *already* walked awhile in *my* shoes.

Maybe we're not so different after all.

On "the future"

I had a dream the other night. I was in the back seat of a car. You were driving. And neither of us knew where the heck we were going ... or if the car would even keep running. That dream pretty much sums up my view of "the future" here at work.

All too often, as an employee I feel like I'm just along for the ride. Sure, I do my part. I wash the windows and pump the gas. But from where I'm sitting, I see the steering wheel in your hands. You may not know where we're headed any more than I do, but at least you're the one driving; you're the one with the most control.

Like most people, I look ahead with a certain amount of fear. I fear that I'll lose more than I'll gain. Will I still have a job or at least be able to find another one if things change here? Will I be able to maintain and improve upon the lifestyle that I enjoy? Will there be health and happiness ahead? Will I be able to handle new technologies and ever-increasing demands? Does management know things they're not telling me? Lots of questions ... very few answers.

I also look ahead with a great deal of hope — hope that my fears will turn out to be unfounded, that things will be even better than they are now. But only time, a little luck, and a lot of hard work will tell.

What's most interesting about my dream is that you and I were in the same car, traveling down the same road. Wherever we go, we go together.

Steer well. And every once in a while, pull over, get out, and walk awhile in *my* shoes.

What I ask of you

Appreciate the fact that my work is no Easier than yours. I've got a tough job, too. Tasks often look easier than they are ... especially when somebody else has to do them.

Don't assume the worst of Me. *You* don't wake up in the morning asking, "How can I make life miserable for someone today?" Well, neither do I. Give me the benefit of the doubt and I will reciprocate.

Continue to Perform your job as best you can. That will make it easier for me to do the same.

Adopt the mindset that to be successful at work, you need me as much as I need you.

Assume half The responsibility for our working relationship. If we work well together, take half the credit. If we don't, accept half the responsibility for making it better. Even though you're the boss, our relationship is a two-way street.

Remember that I'm Human. Before you judge me or decide how you'll deal with me, walk awhile in *my* shoes.

If You do, I think you'll find ...

with more
understanding,
we can meet
in the middle
and walk
the rest of the way
together.

with more
understanding,
we can meet
in the middle
and walk
the rest of the way
together.

What I ask of you

Appreciate the fact that my work is no Easier than yours. I've got a tough job, too. Tasks often look easier than they are ... especially when somebody else has to do them.

Don't assume the worst of Me. *You* don't wake up in the morning asking, "How can I make life miserable for someone today?" Well, neither do I. If you have a problem with something I've done (or haven't done), talk to me about it instead of talking to others.

Continue to Perform your job as best you can. That will make it easier for me to do the same.

Adopt the mindset that to be successful at work, you need me as much as I need you.

Assume half The responsibility for our working relationship. If we work well together, take half the credit. If we don't, accept half the responsibility for making it better.

Remember that I'm Human. Before you judge me or decide how you'll work with me, walk awhile in *my* shoes.

If You do, I think you'll find ...

On "the future"

It used to be I didn't spend much time thinking about the future. Like a lot of people, I just worried about getting through *today* alive and in one piece, figuring I'd focus on crossing tomorrow's bridges when I got to them — *tomorrow*. But things have changed; times have changed. Now I find myself wondering about the future more than ever before.

Sometimes I engage in frivolous dreams — like winning the lottery and living out the rest of my life in the lap of luxury. Yeah, right! In my more rational moments, however, I find myself looking forward with both excitement and anxiety. And that's especially true when it comes to my job.

My excitement stems mostly from the hope that the future will produce many more opportunities for me (and you) to advance, grow, and achieve the fulfillment we all seek. My anxiety comes from the simple fear of the unknown. And, it comes from a deep concern that I may not be able to respond to changes that are happening in business today — concepts like "teams," "empowerment," "re-engineering," and "diversity," to name a few. Some of these will be easy for me to implement and embrace. Others will require great change on my part ... and equally great patience on the part of others — including you.

Do I have all the answers? No. In fact, I usually have more questions than answers. I'll be feeling my way along just like you will. I do, however, know this: The past is gone. The future is all that's left.

Anxious about the future? Walk awhile in *my* shoes.

On the joys of the job

Before you go assuming this book is nothing more than a "woe is me" chronicle, let me set the record straight. There are plenty of joys that come with being a manager. Here are just a few of the "turn-ons" that make the job satisfying for me:

- Doing good work that I can be proud of ... and being recognized and appreciated for it.

- Watching YOU succeed and feeling that I may have had a little something to do with it.

- Meeting — and sometimes beating — deadlines without sacrificing quality or going crazy in the process.

- Finding out from others that you think I'm a decent boss, and, more importantly, a decent person.

- Reflecting on past actions and decisions with the belief that I did the right thing ... no matter how uncomfortable it might have been at the time.

- Making a contribution — feeling that things came out different and better because I was involved.

- Achieving an adequate balance between my job and my personal life.

- Being the messenger of **good news** — downward as well as upward.

When it comes to the above, I'm guessing you feel the same way. No doubt you've *already* walked awhile in *my* shoes.

Maybe we're not so different after all.

The best managers
make decisions on
the basis of what
is fair and equitable,
not what is popular —
bearing in mind
that not everyone
will be pleased with
these decisions.

— Priscilla Gross

On saying "no"

One of the hardest words to say in the English language is "no." It's as hard to say as it is to hear ... sometimes harder. Given my druthers, I'd say yes all the time. Most people would. It makes us feel good when we please others. But you and I both know that's not realistic — it's not always the right thing to do. Somebody has to periodically say no, and I got elected.

When you come to me with a request, an idea, or something else you feel is important, you usually have the luxury of focusing strictly on your issue. I, on the other hand, am stuck with a much bigger picture to look at and evaluate. I have to ask questions like: Can we afford it? How will it affect the work to be done and our priorities? How will it impact other people? Will it be consistent with what I've done with others? What if everybody had the same request? and so on. And what may seem like one simple issue to you may be one of many competing requests or other good ideas I've received that day. You have no way of knowing that ... but I sure do. And I feel bad when I do say no and you walk away disappointed, angry, or both.

So please keep this in mind: I will say yes whenever I can. It certainly won't be every time, but I'll do my best to strike a balance between yeas and nays. And I sure would appreciate it if you'd give me the benefit of the doubt and assume I'm motivated by what's best for *everyone*, because I am. That includes saying no to someone else at times when their request would be unfair to *you*.

Don't like the word "no"? Try walking awhile in *my* shoes.

On personal problems

Most things in life are easier to think and say than they are to do. Such is the case with the common belief that "personal problems should be left at home." I know it's sometimes tough for you to do. I'm just not sure you realize that it's just as tough for me.

When you come to work carrying the excess baggage of family and relationship issues, or maybe health or financial problems, you probably expect a little sensitivity and consideration from me — especially if you've *earned* that consideration through normally good, solid performance. You're right to expect that. And I *do* try to be as sensitive as possible — as long as those problems don't become everyday occurrences. But the real challenge for me is showing concern for you when I'm knee-deep in the same stuff … and doing my best not to let it affect *my* job.

You see, personal problems don't go away when you join management. In fact, it's often just the opposite. You end up with more things to worry about, more things potentially to get you down. And knowing that nobody forced me to take the job doesn't minimize my concerns one bit.

How about showing a little sensitivity to me?! When it comes to personal problems, *my* shoes weigh a ton, too.

When you point
your finger at me,
remember that
three of your fingers
are pointing back
at you!

— Louis Nizer
(adaptation)

On being "objective, consistent, and fair"

At times, I've been accused of being aloof, stand-offish, and downright hard to get to know. Well, I admit it … sometimes I'm guilty as charged. But before you go assuming that I'm an elitist or maybe just plain arrogant, I'd like you to consider the real reason I frequently keep a distance between us: **It's tough to supervise your friends.** If you've ever been placed in a lead worker position, you know exactly what I mean.

"Bosses" inevitably must do things that don't mix well with friendship. Whether it's confronting work problems, doing performance evaluations, or even giving recognition, it's difficult to be objective and fair when dealing with a pal. The more distasteful the task, the greater the likelihood that I'll feel forced to choose between doing my job and keeping a friend. That's a heavy burden for anyone to carry. Making the "right" choice isn't as easy as it might seem.

Equally difficult is meeting the expectation that I be "consistent" and "fair" in my dealings with you. You expect both, and so do *my* bosses. Therein lies the dilemma. **Consistency** basically means treating everyone the same, while **fairness** means treating everyone the way they deserve to be treated based on their particular circumstances. So, since few situations I face are exactly alike, if I'm 100% consistent with everyone, I will inevitably be unfair to someone. And if I'm 100% fair with everyone, I'm consistent with no one; I end up treating people differently. No matter which way I go, somebody's gonna gripe. The best I can do is simply do the best I can do … and somehow try to strike some balance between the two. I work on it every day. Welcome to my world!

Want to know how much easier it is to say "objective, consistent, and fair" than it is to be them? Walk awhile in *my* shoes.

On "no win" situations

Ever feel like you just can't win no matter what you do? Me too! And there's no question it's a lousy feeling.

Perhaps you sometimes feel that way as a result of dealings with me. If that's the case, I acknowledge my responsibility to correct it, because everyone deserves the opportunity to win. But you may not realize that you sometimes make me feel the same way. You occasionally deny me the opportunity to be a winner. And that's equally wrong.

As a manager, I've had my share of "damned if you do and damned if you don't" experiences — especially when it comes to making changes for the better. For example: Let's say you feel I don't adequately recognize your good work. You're understandably upset over something I'm *not* doing. Later, I become aware of this and make a special effort to give you more recognition. But skepticism has set in and you wonder what I'm up to; you assume I have some hidden agenda. Now you're upset that I'm *doing* what it is you wanted in the first place. Result: I lose no matter what. And because I'm only human, eventually I may stop trying altogether … and probably get damned even more.

The only thing worse than losing is being denied the chance to win. Think you're the only one who faces "no win" situations? Walk awhile in *my* shoes.

I never did give anybody hell. I just told the truth and they thought it was hell.

— Harry S. Truman

On dealing with performance problems

Everyone's got something they can identify as the absolute worst part of their job. This is mine. Addressing employee performance problems is the necessary evil of management. I hate it ... it takes a definite toll on me.

Maybe you sometimes think I jump on employees who have problems the first chance I get. Well, I admit I'm not perfect. Perhaps I have reacted too quickly on occasion. But truth be told, I have a greater tendency to put those situations off as long as I can. Sometimes I've avoided confronting problems at all costs — until, that is, they became so serious that I had no choice. That's unfair to you, and for that I apologize. My only explanation for this is that I'm human.

When facing an employee performance problem, I tend to experience two emotions: anxiety and anger. The anxiety comes from just thinking about what I have to do. I don't like telling someone they're not cutting it any more than you do. My guts churn, I get edgy, and I want to put it off *and* get it over with as soon as possible — all at the same time. And then I get angry. I didn't create the problem, the employee did. He or she didn't live up to their responsibilities, and because of that, I have to go through this discomfort. Yet when I meet with the employee, I'm supposed to be calm and businesslike, and follow a ton of guidelines that ensure I handle the issue consistently and fairly. I accept that responsibility, but, trust me, there's nothing easy about it!

Just once, I'd like people to understand and appreciate how tough this is on *me*. When it comes to performance problems, try walking awhile in *my* shoes!

Walk Awhile In *MY* Shoes

Client Priority Code
86R2

Order Form

1-99	$6.95 each	
100-999	$6.45 each	Copies _____
1000-4999	$5.95 each	
5000-9999	$5.45 each	Book Total $ _____
10,000 or more	$4.95 each	

Shipping and Handling*+$ _____

Subtotal $ _____

Texas Only   Sales Tax (8.25% of Subtotal) $ _____

TOTAL $ _____

---

*SHIPPING & HANDLING CHARGES:

Order $ Amount	Charges
Up to $50	$4
$50-99	$7
$100-249	$10
$250-649	$18
$650-1,299	$32
$1,300-1,999	$55
$2,000-3,499	$68

Outside the continental U.S., please call.

Orders shipped ground delivery to be received in 7-10 business days. Next business day and second business day delivery is available. Please call for information.

☐ YES, I want more information on WALK THE TALK® Workshops, Consulting, and 360° Profile Services to help my organization turn values into value-added results. Please send me a free WALK THE TALK® RESOURCES Catalog.

Name (MR/MS) _____

Title _____

Organization _____

Street Address _____

City _____ State _____ Zip _____ Country _____

Phone ( ) _____ Ext. _____ (required to process order)

Fax ( ) _____ E-mail _____

Purchase Order Number (if applicable) _____

☐ MasterCard   ☐ VISA   ☐ AMERICAN EXPRESS **Cards**   ☐ Check or Money Order Enclosed (Payable to: The WALK THE TALK Co.)   ☐ Please Invoice (orders over $100 only)

Account Number _____ Expiration Date _____
(month/year)

Signature _____

Prices effective January 1, 1998 are subject to change without notice. Orders payable in U.S. dollars only. Orders outside U.S. and Canada must be prepaid by credit card or check drawn on a U.S. bank. Orders under $100 must be prepaid by credit card, check, or money order. Restocking fee on returns within 30 days of original receipt. THANK YOU FOR YOUR ORDER.

TO ORDER

☎ **1.888.822.WALK (9255)**

📠 972.243.0815

Ask about our other high high-impact publications:

◆ *Walk The Talk ... And Get The Results You Want*
The best-selling business book that shows leaders, at all
levels, why and how to turn organizational values into value-
added practices.

◆ *144 Ways To Walk The Talk*
The quick-reference handbook packed with practical ideas
and strategies for practicing values-driven leadership.

◆ *Walking The Talk Together*
The powerful handbook that encourages all employees to
take responsibility for values-driven business practices.

◆ *Forget For Success*
The practical, easy-read that pinpoints counterproductive
beliefs and people practices which negatively impact your
culture and bottom line.

For information on these and other values-based
business resources, visit our website:

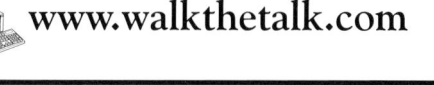 **www.walkthetalk.com**

Values Based Business Solutions

The WALK THE TALK® Company
2925 LBJ Freeway, Suite 201, Dallas, Texas 75234-7100
972.243.8863 ▸ Fax 972.243.0815 ▸ www.walkthetalk.com

By working faithfully
eight hours a day,
   you may eventually
      get to be boss
and work
      twelve hours a day!

— Robert Frost

On the "privileges" of management

There's no denying that I occasionally enjoy certain benefits and freedoms that you don't.

Granted, I'm usually not held to the same work schedule as you. Sometimes I may take longer lunches than you are allowed. Some days I arrive later or leave earlier than normal. And yes, once in a while I have an opportunity to mix business with pleasure — something that's rarely afforded to you. Undoubtedly, you're aware of other management "privileges" as well. You see them happening, and they probably tick you off, right? Sure! It's only natural. What you may not realize, however, is that the few special benefits I enjoy balance out with the things I do that you *don't* see and therefore don't know about.

How could you know? You're not here every time I come in early to keep up with the day's work. You're not here every time I stay late for supposedly short meetings that never are. You're not here every time I work on my days off in order to meet yet another deadline. And you have no idea how many times, out of business necessity, I must once again place work ahead of family, friends, and personal enjoyment.

If, as some people say, "rank has its privileges," it can only be because "rank" also has its extra demands. Both come with the job. But I guarantee you there are more demands than there are privileges. And of those privileges I do enjoy, overtime pay *isn't* one of them.

The next time you get angry about a management perk, try switching roles. Are you absolutely sure you'd do things differently if you walked awhile in *my* shoes?

On selection
and promotion

When it comes to selecting people for promotions, special assignments, or the like, it's tough to win. Tough, that is, if I pay any attention to what the candidates think.

Here's the scenario: Ten people are competing for one promotion. No matter who I choose, one person is going to feel I made the right decision, and the other nine are gonna think I screwed up. If *you're* the one who gets selected, you'll probably suggest that I pay no attention to what the others think. Of course, if you *aren't* selected, you'll undoubtedly question my motives in making a selection that so many people think is wrong. Get the picture?

There's a lot more to selection decisions than you might think. Sometimes it may seem that I merely pick the people I like. Well, here's a shocker for you: It's true! But who I "like" is determined by weighing many factors, such as technical skills, people skills, what we need now, what we'll need in the future, past performance, seniority, diversity considerations, interest, ability, and much more. You don't have to use those same criteria in determining who *you* like.

So, if you're ever tempted to second guess my selection and promotion decisions, remember this simple fact: I have to live with the people I pick just as you do. There's no way I'd select someone I didn't feel could handle the job well.

When it comes to selection and promotion, take *my* shoes ... please!

It's much safer to obey than to rule.

— Thomas à Kempis

On evaluating employee performance

I admit it. I have a love/hate attitude about performance evaluations. I love it when you do great work and I get to tell you, and perhaps reward you for your contributions. On the other hand, I hate it when you don't do great work, and I not only have to tell you, but also deal with your objections, disappointment, and even hostility.

Doing performance evaluations is a basic responsibility of management. It's necessary to ensure we all get the feedback we need to keep our performance on track. But it's a part of the job I'm not always comfortable with. Think it's easy to play judge and jury over someone else's work? Trust me, it isn't — especially if *my* assessment affects *your* salary ... and your future. And the more people I have to appraise, the tougher it gets. Lots of second guessing myself; lots of rules and parameters to follow; lots of writer's cramp; and sometimes lots of heated discussion.

Most people think they do great work. Many of them are right ... but not all of them. In the end, I *must* call it like I see it. That's all I can do.

That's all you could do if you walked awhile in *my* shoes.

On how you perceive me

Someone once said, "If you want to be liked, don't become a boss." They were right! You just can't please everyone. If I've learned anything, it's that no matter what I do, inevitably somebody's gonna be chapped. That's a reality that comes with the job. I accept it. But there's another reality I'd like you to know about — a reality that comes with being human: I care what you and others think of me.

Do I sometimes *act* like I don't care? Sure! But with few exceptions, it's just that — an act. You see, convincing myself that I don't care (or at least trying to) gets me through difficult situations. It's what helps me follow through on what I believe to be right when the right thing is also the unpopular thing. If you're a parent, you undoubtedly understand what I'm saying.

I especially care what you think about me when it comes to honesty, integrity, and fairness. I'll bet you consider yourself a fair person. You probably take pride in that. Well, so do I. But occasionally I get a bum rap for being unfair in my dealings with employees. You hear one side of the story — without all the facts — and form an opinion about me. I know it and it bothers me, but I can't defend myself because the facts are usually confidential. So I take the rap … and pretend I don't care. But I do.

I fully understand that I must *earn* your trust and respect just as you must earn mine. And I'm working to do that. As I work on it, maybe you could give me the same benefit of the doubt that you would wish from me.

Before you judge me, try walking awhile in *my* shoes!